UNIVERSAL EDITION

Alfred's Basic Piano Li...

Piano

Lesson Book
Level 1B

Correlated materials to be used with *Lesson Book, Level 1B:*

*Teacher's discretion.

**May be used upon completion of Lesson Book 1B, before the student begins Lesson Book 2.

A General MIDI disk (8583) and a Compact Disc (14543) are available, which include a full piano recording and background accompaniment.

Theory Games Software correlating to Levels 1A–5 is available for Macintosh and IBM/Windows-compatible computers.

Willard A. Palmer • Morton Manus • Amanda Vick Lethco

Second Edition
Copyright © MCMXCV by Alfred Publishing Co., Inc.
ISBN 0-7390-0664-9

Illustrations by David Silverman (Painted by Cheryl Hennigar)

Review

THE GRAND STAVE

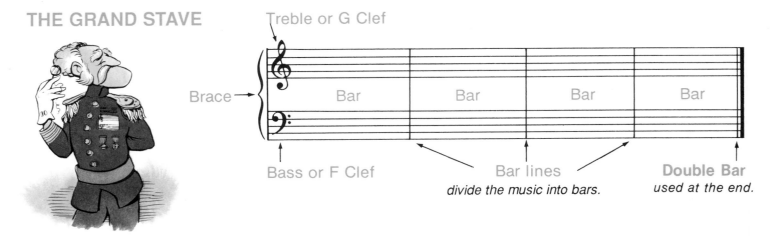

Treble or G Clef

Brace →

Bar   Bar   Bar   Bar

Bass or F Clef

Bar lines

divide the music into bars.

Double Bar
used at the end.

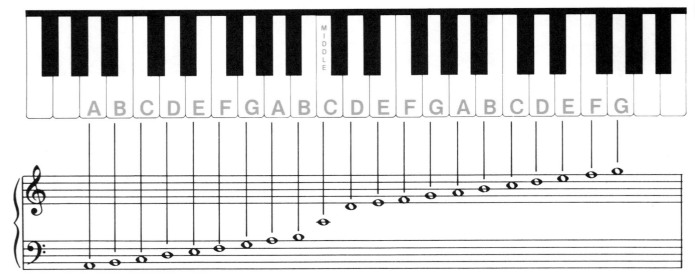

A B C D E F G A B C D E F G A B C D E F G

> **DYNAMIC SIGNS** tell how LOUD or SOFT to play.
>
> ***mf*** (MEZZO FORTE) = *MODERATELY LOUD*

TIME SIGNATURE

4/4 means **4** beats to each bar.

a **CROTCHET** ♩ gets ONE beat.

NOTE VALUES

♩ = CROTCHET
COUNT "1"

♩ = MINIM
COUNT "1 - 2"

○ = SEMIBREVE
COUNT "1 - 2 - 3 - 4"

REST VALUES

𝄽 = CROTCHET REST
COUNT "1"

▬ = MINIM REST
COUNT "1 - 2"

▬ = SEMIBREVE REST
COUNT "1 - 2 - 3 - 4"
(or rest for a whole bar)

You are now ready to begin THEORY BOOK and NOTESPELLER, Level 1B.

C Position Review

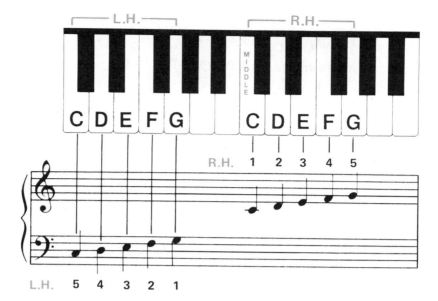

Play and say the note names.

1. Clap (or tap) & count.   2. Play & count.   3. Play & sing the words.
Follow these steps for each piece in this book!

Step Right Up!

Moderately Slow

1. Step right up to   tre - ble G,   Then step left to   mid - dle C.
2. "C   D   E   F   G   G   G,   G   F   E   D   C   C   C.

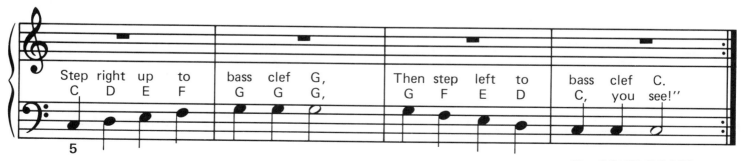

Step right up to   bass clef G,   Then step left to   bass clef C.
C   D   E   F   G   G   G,   G   F   E   D   C, clef you see!"

The DOUBLE DOTS mean REPEAT FROM THE BEGINNING.

Review—Melodic Intervals

Distances between notes are measured in **INTERVALS,** called 2nds, 3rds, 4ths, 5ths, etc.

Notes played **SEPARATELY** make a **MELODY.**
We call the intervals between these notes **MELODIC INTERVALS.**

Play these MELODIC INTERVALS. Listen to the sound of each interval.

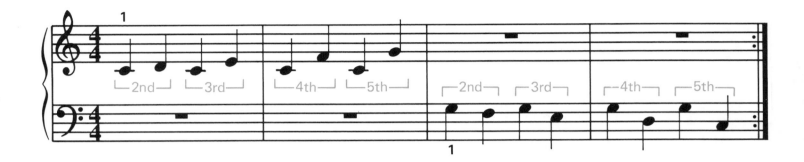

The Carousel

Name all the MELODIC INTERVALS
in this piece before you play it.

Brightly

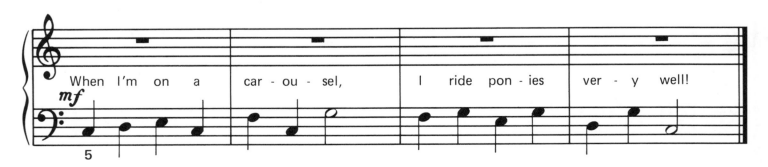

Let's Go to America!

SLUR means play **LEGATO** (smoothly connected).

Majestically

1. Let's go to A - mer - i - ca! Far a - cross the o - cean.
2. Let's go to A - mer - i - ca! Set the ship in mo - tion!

SLURS often divide the music into phrases (musical thoughts).

Brother John

| p (PIANO) = *SOFT* | f (FORTE) = *LOUD* |

Moderately fast

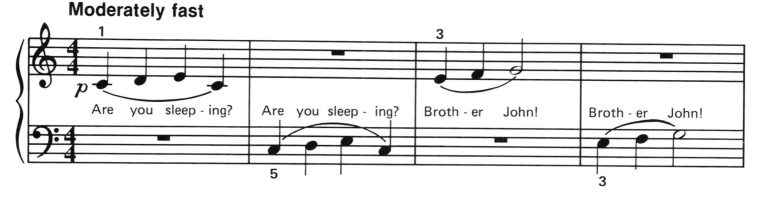

Are you sleep - ing? Are you sleep - ing? Broth - er John! Broth - er John!

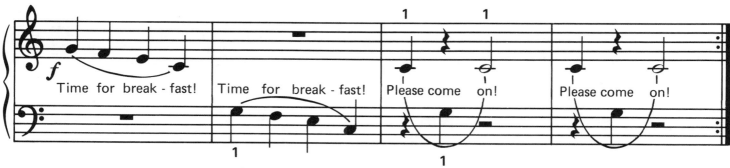

Time for break - fast! Time for break - fast! Please come on! Please come on!

You are now ready to begin SIGHT READING FOLK SONGS and TECHNIC BOOK, Level 1B.

Review—Harmonic Intervals

Notes played TOGETHER make HARMONY.
We call the intervals between these notes **HARMONIC INTERVALS.**

Play these HARMONIC INTERVALS. Listen carefully to the sound of each interval.

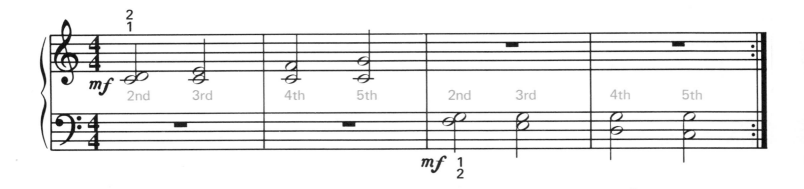

Good Sounds

Moderately fast

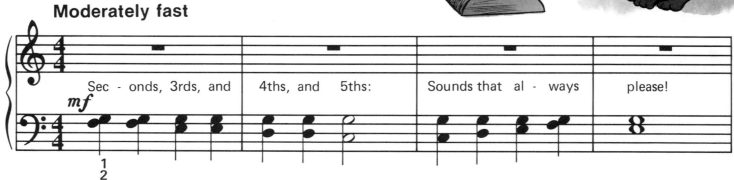

Sec - onds, 3rds, and   4ths, and   5ths: Sounds that al - ways   please!

Sec - onds, 3rds, and   4ths, and   5ths   Make great har - mo - nies!

You are now ready to begin HYMN BOOK and RECITAL BOOK, Level 1B.

TIME SIGNATURE (REVIEW)

3 means **3** beats to each bar.

4 a **CROTCHET** ♩ gets ONE beat.

𝅗𝅥. = **DOTTED MINIM**   COUNT "1 - 2 - 3"

The Cuckoo

First play the left hand alone, naming each HARMONIC INTERVAL.

Happily

1. Cuck - oo,   cuck - oo,   sing - ing so   near!
2. Cuck - oo,   cuck - oo,   sing - ing so   clear!

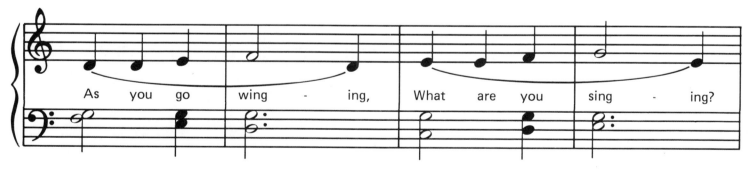

As   you   go   wing - ing,   What   are   you   sing - ing?

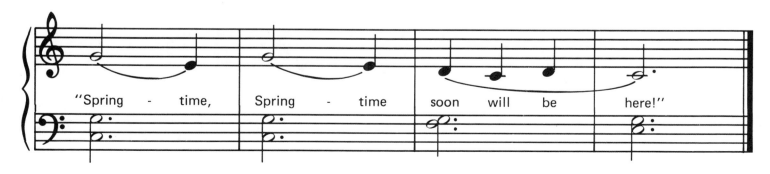

"Spring - time,   Spring - time   soon   will   be   here!"

You are now ready to begin Ear Training Book, Level 1B.

REVIEWING THE **SHARP SIGN**

The SHARP SIGN
before a note means
play the next key to the right,
whether BLACK or WHITE.

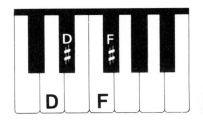

When a SHARP SIGN appears before a note,
it applies to that note for the rest of the bar.

Money Can't Buy Ev'rything!

March time

Mon - ey can't buy ev - 'ry - thing! Mon - ey can't make you a king.

Mon - ey may not bring suc - cess; Mon - ey can't buy hap - pi - ness!

But of one thing I am sure: Mon - ey does - n't make you poor.

Mon - ey does - n't make you sad; Mon - ey can't be all that bad!

You are now ready to begin DUET BOOK and FUN SOLO BOOK, Level 1B.

STACCATO (REVIEW)

STACCATO is the opposite of LEGATO. It means SEPARATED or DETACHED.
To play STACCATO, *release* the key instantly.

STACCATO is indicated by a DOT over or under the note.

Ping-Pong

Brightly

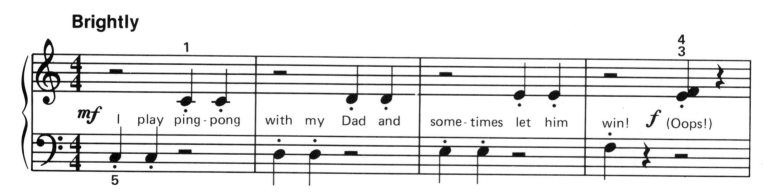

mf I play ping-pong with my Dad and some-times let him win! *f* (Oops!)

mf When he hits the ball too hard I fetch it back a - gain! *f* (Out!)

Grandpa's Clock

INCOMPLETE BAR

Some pieces begin with an INCOMPLETE BAR. The 1st bar in this piece has only ONE count. The three missing counts are found in the last bar. When you repeat the whole piece, you will have one whole bar of 4 counts when you play the last bar plus the first bar.

Moderately fast

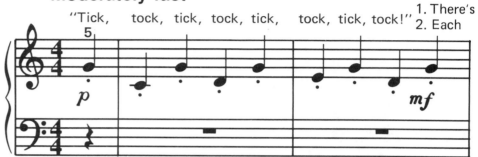

not a clock in our whole block that
hour it dings and dongs and rings. It

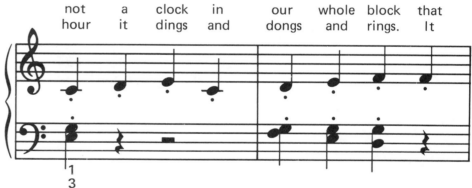

stands as tall as Grand-pa's clock! Out in the hall it
has a pen-du - lum that swings, And all day long it

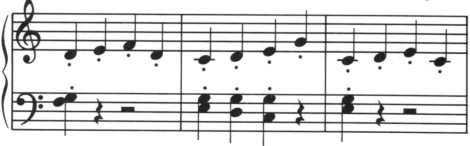

sings, "Tick, tock! Tick, tock! Tick, tock!"
stands and sings, "Tick, tock! Tick, tock!"

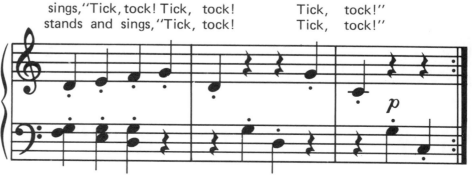

When the Saints Go Marching In

March time

Oh, when the Saints go march-ing in,

Oh, when the Saints go march-ing in,

How I want to join that num-ber,

When the Saints go march-ing in!

G Position Review

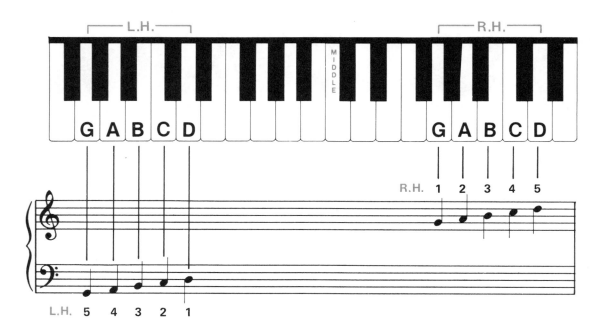

Play and say the note names.

G's in the "BAG"

Moderately fast

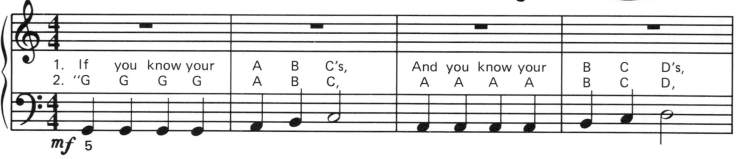

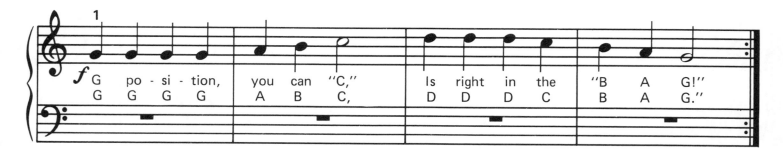

REVIEW: DYNAMIC SIGNS

CRESCENDO *(gradually louder)*   DIMINUENDO *(gradually softer)*

Join the Fun

Moderately fast

mf Ev - 'ry - one | join the fun! | Laugh and sing your | cares a - way!

Come and play, | ev - 'ry day! | We will have such | fun!

p We'll go swim-ming | in the sound, | *mf* That's where laugh-ter's | al - ways found.

f Come with me! | You will see! | We'll have lots of | fun!

14

This is an **ACCENT SIGN.**

> When there is an ACCENT SIGN
over or under a note,
play that note LOUDER.

Oom-Pa-pa!

Moderately fast

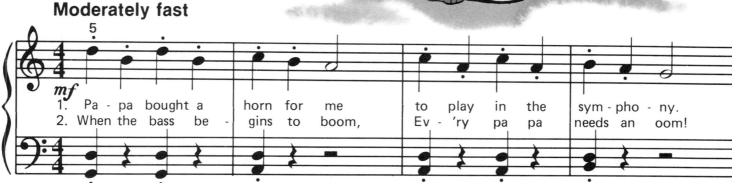

1. Pa - pa bought a horn for me to play in the sym - pho - ny.
2. When the bass be - gins to boom, Ev - 'ry pa pa needs an oom!

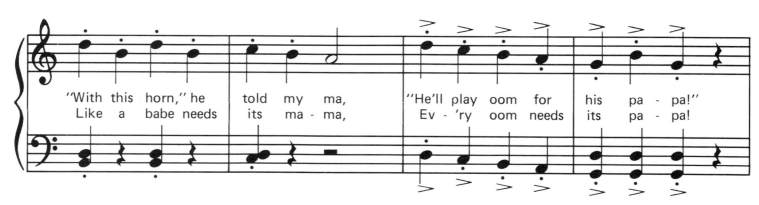

"With this horn," he told my ma, "He'll play oom for his pa - pa!"
Like a babe needs its ma - ma, Ev - 'ry oom needs its pa - pa!

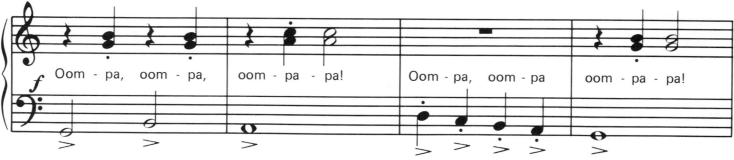

Oom - pa, oom - pa, oom - pa - pa! Oom - pa, oom - pa oom - pa - pa!

Oom - pa, oom - pa, oom - pa - pa! "He'll play oom for his pa - pa!"
Ev - 'ry oom needs its pa - pa!

Suggestion: After playing the entire piece twice, repeat the last 2 lines, again,
playing the L.H. one octave lower!

REVIEWING THE **FLAT SIGN**

The FLAT SIGN before a note means play the next key to the left, whether BLACK or WHITE.

When a FLAT SIGN appears before a note, it applies to that note for the rest of the bar.

The Clown

Moderately fast

mf

See the fun - ny, fun - ny clown. He climbs up and he falls down!

You will nev - er see him frown! He's a fun - ny clown.

Fine

f

Al - ways be a glad clown! Al - ways steal the show!

p

When you are a sad clown, nev - er let us know.

D.C. al Fine

D.C. al Fine (Da Capo al Fine) means repeat from the beginning and play to the end **(Fine)**.

Reading in Middle C Position

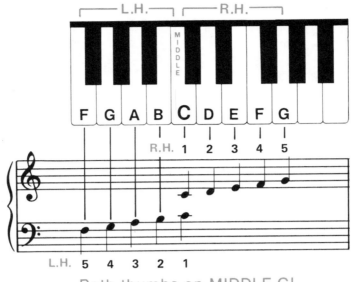

Both thumbs on MIDDLE C!

Play and say the note names.

NEW NOTES

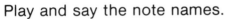

Thumbs on C!

Moderately slow

1. Left hand thumb on mid - dle C! Just three new notes. A B C.
2. F G A B C C C, C B A A A B C.

mf

5

Right hand thumb on mid - dle C! Same notes as po - si - tion C.
G F E D C C C, C D E D C C C.

mf

5

Tempo Marks

TEMPO is an Italian word. It means "RATE OF SPEED."
Words indicating the rate of speed used in
playing music are called **TEMPO MARKS.**
Here are some of the most important tempo marks:

ALLEGRO = Quickly, happily.
MODERATO = Moderately.
ANDANTE = Moving along. The word actually means "walking."
ADAGIO = Slowly.

Waltz Time

MIDDLE C POSITION

Bring out the LH melody.

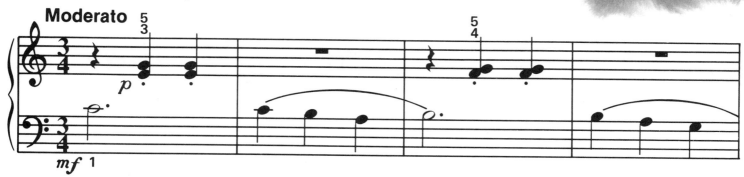

Suggestion: Repeat with both hands one octave higher.

Good King Wenceslas

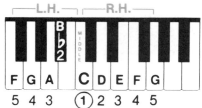

Allegro moderato (moderately fast)

Good King Wen - ces - las look'd out, On the feast of Ste - phen,

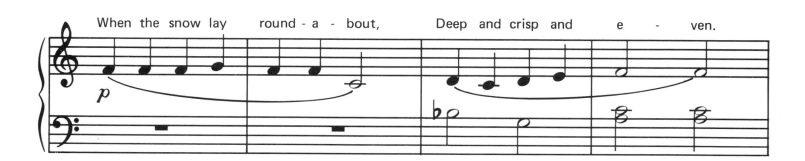

When the snow lay round - a - bout, Deep and crisp and e - ven.

Bright - ly shone the moon that night, Though the frost was cru - el,

When a poor man came in sight, Gath-'ring win - ter fu - el.

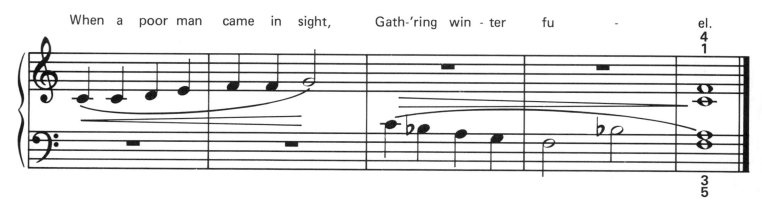

The Rainbow

This sign is called a **PAUSE.**

Hold the note under the PAUSE longer than its value.

Roy G. Biv*

* Remember the name "Roy G. Biv" and you will always know the colours of the rainbow
in the order in which they appear.

Good Morning to You!

Allegro (quickly, happily)

Good morn - ing to you! Good

morn - ing to you! Good morn - ing, Dear

_____! Good morn - ing to you!
(name)

Quavers or Eighth Notes

Two quavers are played in the time of **one crotchet.**

When a piece contains quavers,
count: "one-and" for each crotchet;
count: "one-and" for each pair of quavers.

Clap (or tap) these notes, counting aloud.

Happy Birthday to You!

HAPPY BIRTHDAY is exactly the same as *GOOD MORNING TO YOU,*
except for the QUAVERS!

A NEW TIME SIGNATURE

2 means **2** beats to each bar.

4 a **crotchet** gets ONE beat.

Clap (or tap) the following rhythm.
Clap **ONCE** for each note, counting aloud.

Yankee Doodle

A SEMIBREVE REST is used to indicate a whole bar
of silence in 2/4 time.

Allegro moderato

Yan - kee Doo - dle   went to town,   Rid - ing on a   po - ny He

stuck a feath - er   in his hat and   called it mac - a - ro - ni!

DUET PART: (Student plays 1 octave higher.)

The Windmill

Andante

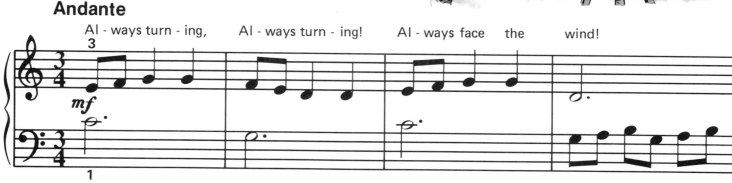

Al - ways turn - ing,   Al - ways turn - ing!   Al - ways face the   wind!

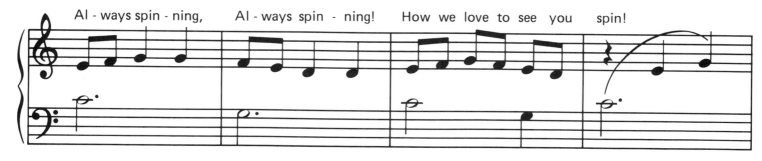

Al - ways spin - ning,   Al - ways spin - ning!   How we love to see you   spin!

When the wind is   blow - ing, and   ev - en when it's   slow - ing,

rit - - - - - - - ar - - - - - dan - - - - - do

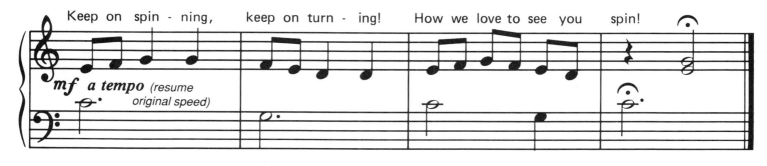

Keep on spin - ning,   keep on turn - ing!   How we love to see you   spin!

a tempo (resume original speed)

Suggestion: For recital performance, repeat *THE WINDMILL* playing both hands
one octave higher; then play the last line AGAIN, very slowly and softly.

Indians

G POSITION

Moderato

1. Cher-o-kee, Chick-a-saw, Chat-ta-wa, Chip-pe-wa, too,_____
2. Kick-a-poo, Ki-o-wa, Ot-ta-wa, I-o-wa, Sioux._____

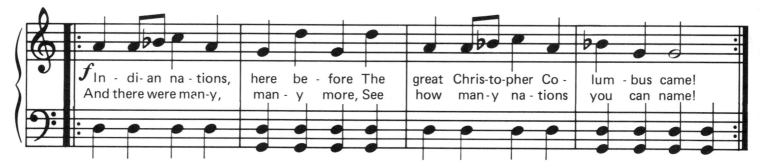

f In - di-an na - tions, here be - fore The great Chris-to-pher Co - lum - bus came!
And there were man-y, man - y more, See how man-y na - tions you can name!

mf Paw-nee, A - ra-pa-ho, Shaw-nee, and Nav-a - ho, too._____

p _____ rit - - - - - - - - - ar - - - - - - - - - dan - - - - - - - - - - - - - do

Note: *Sioux* is pronounced "Soo." It rhymes with "too."

The double dots inside the double bars indicate
that everything between the double bars must be REPEATED.

G Position with L.H. an Octave Higher

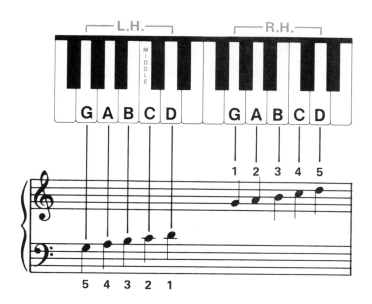

In this NEW G POSITION, the LEFT HAND plays ONE OCTAVE HIGHER than before. The RIGHT HAND remains in the same position.

There is only ONE new L.H. note to learn.

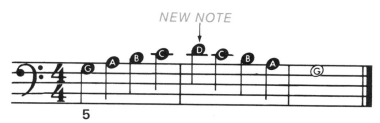

New Position G

Moderato

mf

1. G,   G,   Gee what fun,   play - ing   up   to   D!
2. "G   G   G   A   B,   B   A   B   C   D,

G,   the mu - sic   sounds so   good   in   new po - si - tion   G!
G   G   D   D   B   B   G   G   D   C   B   A   G."

The Damper Pedal

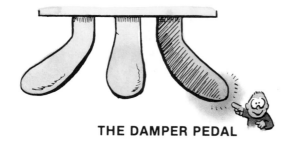

THE DAMPER PEDAL

The RIGHT PEDAL is called the **DAMPER PEDAL.**

When you hold the damper pedal down, any note you sound continues after you release the key.

The RIGHT FOOT is used on the damper pedal. Always keep your heel on the floor; use your ankle like a hinge.

This sign shows when the damper pedal is to be used:

This sign means: PEDAL DOWN

HOLD PEDAL — PEDAL UP

Pedal Play

This easy PEDAL STUDY will show you how the damper pedal causes the notes to continue to sound, EVEN AFTER YOUR HANDS HAVE RELEASED THE KEYS.

Press the pedal down as you play each group of notes. Hold it down through the rests.

Play **VERY SLOWLY** and **LISTEN.**

Harp Song

VERY IMPORTANT!
Also play *HARP SONG* in the following ways:

1. Play the 3rd and 4th bar of each line one octave higher than written.
2. Play the 1st and 2nd bar of each line one octave lower than written.
3. Any combination of the above 2 ways.

Concert Time

8va — The sign, **8va** placed over the notes, means PLAY THE NOTES ONE OCTAVE (8 NOTES) HIGHER THAN WRITTEN.

Allegro Moderato

BOTH HANDS 8va

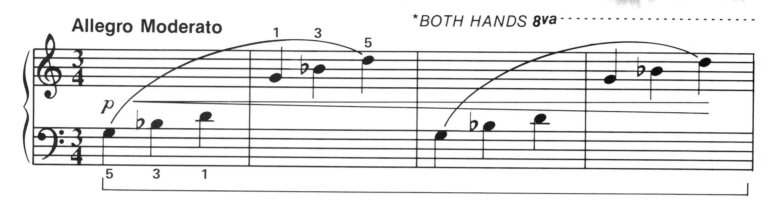

BOTH HANDS *8va*

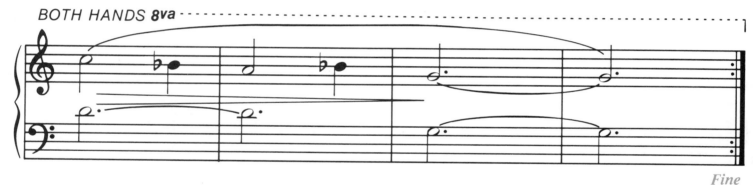

Fine

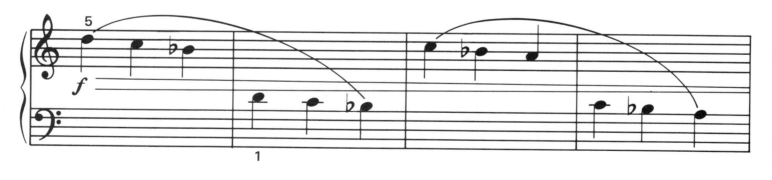

D.C. al Fine

*8va applies only to the STAVE below it unless "both hands" is added.

Music Box Rock

Allegro

*Play both hands **8va** throughout.*

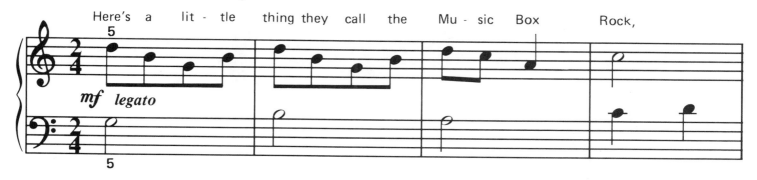

Here's a lit-tle thing they call the Mu-sic Box Rock,

mf legato

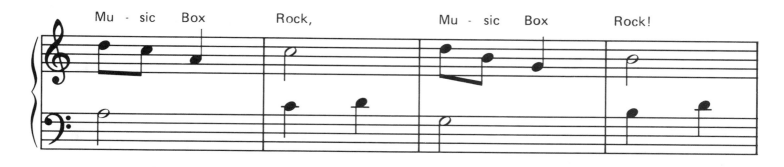

Mu-sic Box Rock, Mu-sic Box Rock!

Wind a lit-tle spring and it-'ll run like a clock;

last time ritardando to end

Let it play un-til it runs down.

Repeat as many times as you like!

A Cowboy's Song

A special WESTERN EFFECT may be produced by playing the pairs
of quavers a bit unevenly, in a "lilting" style:

long   short   long   short, etc.

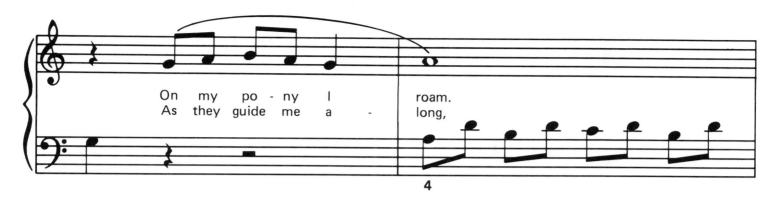

On my po - ny I roam.
As they guide me a - long,

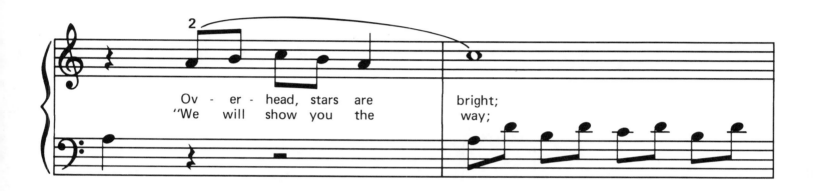

Ov - er - head, stars are bright;
"We will show you the way;

I'm a long way from home!
We won't let you go wrong!"

rit - - - - - ar - - - - - dan - - - - - do - - - - - - - - - - - -   *p*

Suggestion: Play *A COWBOY'S SONG* also with L.H. **8va lower**, in the old G position.

This is a **QUAVER REST.**

It means REST FOR THE VALUE OF A QUAVER.

When quavers appear singly, they look like this: or

Single quavers are often used with quaver rests.

COUNT: "one-and"

Clap (or tap) the following rhythm:

The Magic Man

Mysteriously

1. Who can pull a rab - bit out of
2. Who can van - ish an - y - thing and

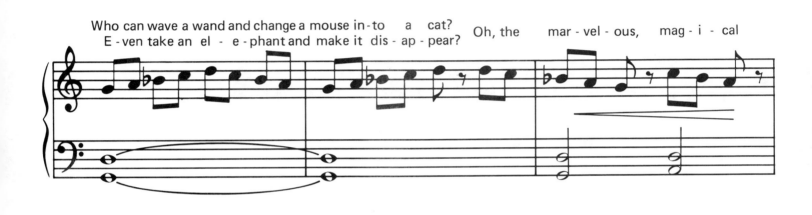

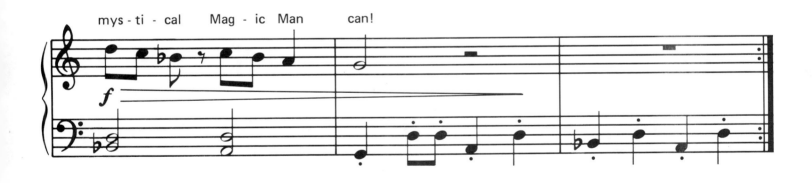

Middle D Position

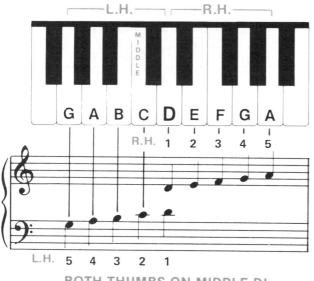

BOTH THUMBS ON MIDDLE D!
L.H. same as new G Position.

The Greatest Show on Earth!

March Tempo

Come to the Great-est show on Earth!_____ It's full of

fun!_____ It's full of mirth!_____ Come see the

clowns and tum-blers too;_____ See what our

ac - ro - bats can do!_____ And when the

mus - ic starts to play,_____ You'll say "Hoo -

ray!_____ It's Cir - cus Day!_____ And you will

shout for all you're worth,_____ "Come to the

Great - est Show on Earth!"

Measuring Semitones

A **SEMITONE** or **HALF STEP** is the distance from any key to the very next key up or down, black or white, with **NO KEY BETWEEN.**

The SHARP sign ♯ raises a note a half step.

The FLAT sign ♭ lowers a note a half step.

Each black key may be named 2 ways, as shown here:

The NATURAL sign ♮ is used to **CANCEL** a sharp or a flat.
A note after a natural is **ALWAYS a WHITE KEY!**

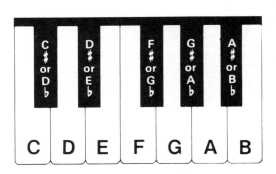

Middle D "Half Step" Position

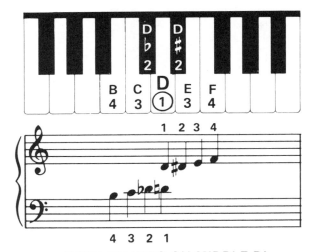

BOTH THUMBS ON MIDDLE D!

PLAY & COUNT:

The Whirlwind

MIDDLE D "SEMITONE" POSITION

This piece consists entirely of semitones, except for the last 2 bars.

Allegro moderato

1. Whist - ling, whirl - ing, twist - ing, turn - ing, Soar - ing, swirl - ing, chas - ing, churn - ing,
2. Whip - ping, whisk - ing, curv - ing, curl - ing, Flit - ting, frisk - ing, hum - ming, hurl - ing

Swift - ly swerv - ing, circ - ling, send - ing Leaves in live - ly spi - rals spin - ning.
Puffs of fluff and down of thist - les, How it huffs and howls and whist - les!

Diz - zi - ly it winds and chas - es Ev - 'ry - thing it finds and rac - es

(Cross L.H. over R.H.)

rit - - - - - - - - ar - - - - - - - - - - dan - - - - do

Whirl - ing, twirl - ing, swirl - ing out of sight!

Measuring Whole Tones

A **WHOLE TONE** or **WHOLE STEP** is equal to 2 SEMITONES with **ONE KEY BETWEEN.**

Middle D "Whole Tone" Position

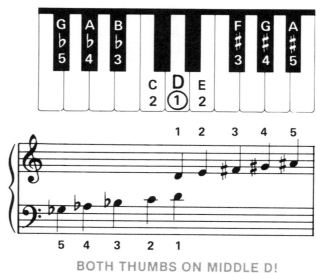

BOTH THUMBS ON MIDDLE D!

When a SHARP or FLAT appears before a note, it applies to that note each time it is used in the rest of the bar, unless it is cancelled by a natural.

A SHARP or FLAT continues when a note is tied to the following bar.
It is not necessary to re-write the sharp or flat before the 2nd of the two tied notes.

PLAY & COUNT:

The Planets

MIDDLE D "WHOLE TONE" POSITION

Andante

1. Mer - cu - ry, Ve - nus, and Earth, and then Mars;
2. Ju - pi - ter, Sat - urn, and U - ra - nus, too;

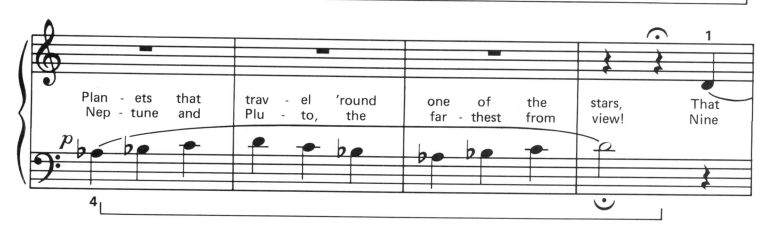

Plan - ets that trav - el 'round one of the stars, That
Nep - tune and Plu - to, round the far - thest the from view! Nine

blaz - ing star we call the Sun.
plan - ets trav - 'ling 'round the Sun.

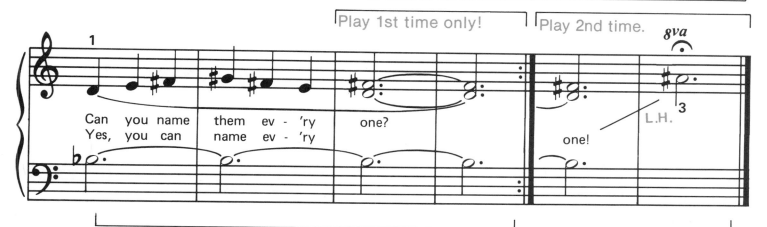

Play 1st time only! | Play 2nd time.

Can you name them ev - 'ry one?
Yes, you can name ev - 'ry one!

Tetrachords

A TETRACHORD is a series of FOUR NOTES having a pattern of

WHOLE TONE, WHOLE TONE, SEMITONE

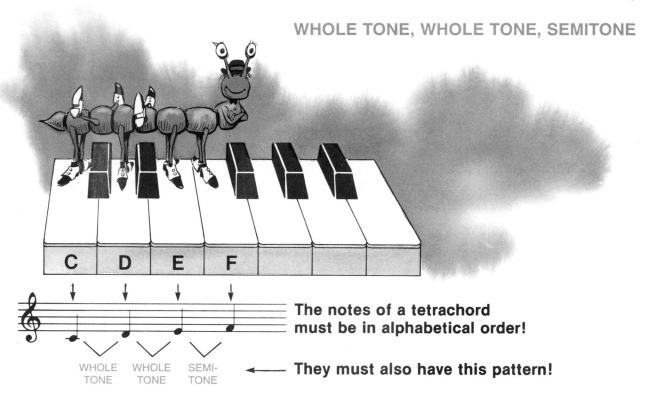

The notes of a tetrachord must be in alphabetical order!

← **They must also have this pattern!**

PLAY THE FOLLOWING TETRACHORDS.

L.H. tetrachords are fingered **5 4 3 2.**

R.H. tetrachords are fingered **2 3 4 5.**

C TETRACHORDS:

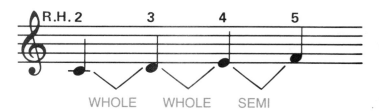

G TETRACHORDS:

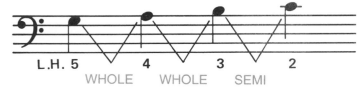

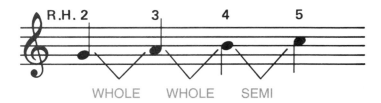

D TETRACHORDS:

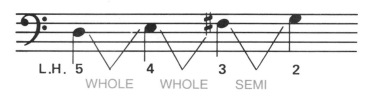

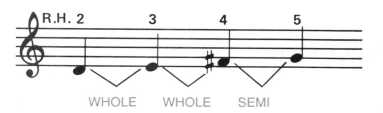

The Major Scale

The MAJOR SCALE is made of **TWO TETRACHORDS** *joined* by a **WHOLE TONE**.

THE C MAJOR SCALE

> *There is NO ♯ or ♭ in the* **C MAJOR SCALE**.

Each scale begins and ends on a note of the same name as the scale, called the **KEY NOTE** or **TONIC**.

C Major Scale Piece

Both 5's play the **KEY-NOTE, C!**

1. Play whole, whole, semi. Play whole, whole, semi. Then come down the ver - y same way!
2. Watch the semi - tones! Watch the semi - tones! Tet - ra - chords are eas - y to play!

THE G MAJOR SCALE

> *There is ONE ♯ (F♯) in the* **G MAJOR SCALE**.

G Major Scale Piece

Both 5's play the **KEY-NOTE, G!**

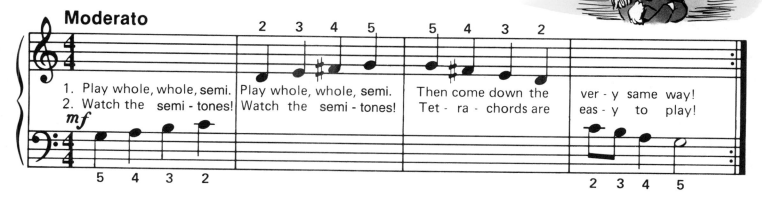

Moderato

1. Play whole, whole, semi. Play whole, whole, semi. Then come down the ver - y same way!
2. Watch the semi - tones! Watch the semi - tones! Tet - ra - chords are eas - y to play!

42

The Key of G Major

A piece based on the G Major scale is in the **KEY OF G MAJOR**.
Since F is sharp in the G scale, every F is sharp.

Instead of placing a sharp before every F,
the sharp is indicated at the beginning in the KEY SIGNATURE.

Carol in G Major

HAND POSITION: R.H. plays the upper tetrachord, L.H. plays the lower tetrachord.

KEY OF G MAJOR
Key Signature: one sharp (F♯)
Play all "F's" sharp throughout.

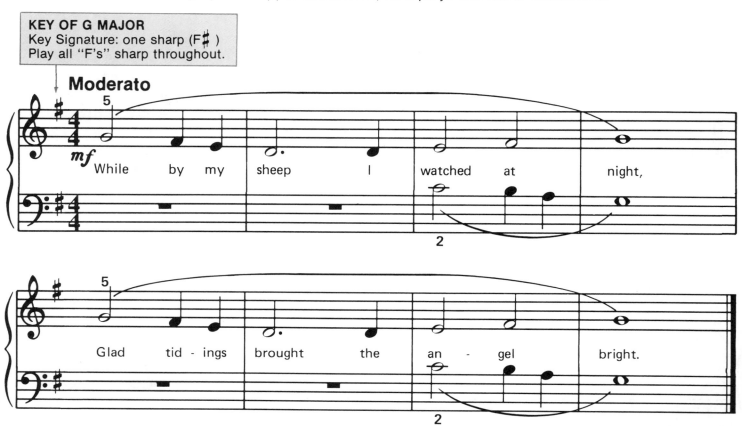

The Same Carol in C Major

HAND POSITION: R.H. plays the upper tetrachord, L.H. plays the lower tetrachord.

KEY OF C MAJOR
Key Signature: no ♯, no ♭.

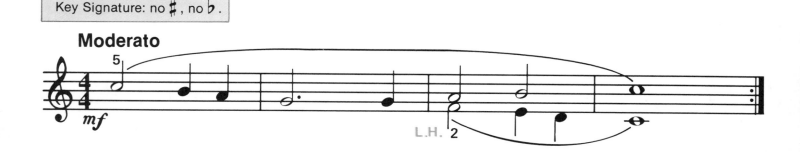

A Piece with 2 L.H. Positions

L.H. C POSITION
Line 3

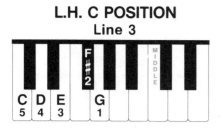

L.H. G POSITION
Lines 1, 2

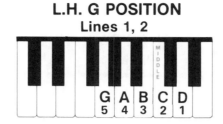

R.H. POSITION

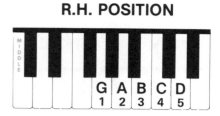

From the KEY SIGNATURE you will see that this piece is in the KEY OF G MAJOR—
all F's must be SHARPENED. Watch for the F's in the L.H. part of the last line!

French Lullaby

A Piece with 2 R.H. Positions

L.H. C POSITION

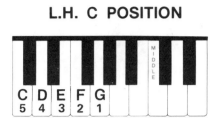

R.H. C POSITION
Lines 1–4

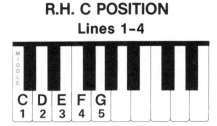

R.H. G POSITION
Lines 5, 6

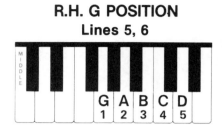

The piece begins in the KEY OF C MAJOR, changes to the KEY OF G MAJOR, then returns to C MAJOR. Be sure to make all the F's sharp in the 5th and 6th lines.

Sonatina

KEY OF C MAJOR
no #, no ♭.

Allegro moderato

A *SONATINA* is a short instrumental selection. It may have one, two, or three movements. If the first or only movement begins in the key of C major, the second part of the movement is usually in the key of G major. The movement returns to the original key at the end.

2nd time ritardando (Move R.H. to G POSITION)

Fine

KEY OF G MAJOR
1♯ (F♯)

mf

(Move R.H. to C POSITION)

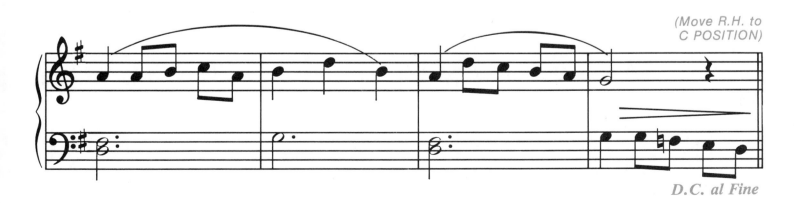

D.C. al Fine

This piece is in the **KEY OF C MAJOR.** Although there are no sharps or flats in the key signature, some sharps occur during the piece. Sharps or flats not in the key signature are called *accidentals.*

When Our Band Goes Marching By!

C POSITION

Review of Musical Terms

Accent (>) — placed over or under a note that gets special emphasis. Play the note louder.

Accidental — a sharp or flat not given in the key signature.

Adagio — slowly.

Allegro — quickly, happily.

Andante — moving along (at walking speed).

A tempo — resume original speed.

Crescendo (————————) — gradually louder.

Da Capo al Fine (D.C. al Fine) — repeat from the beginning and play to the Fine (end).

Diminuendo (————————) — gradually softer.

Dynamic signs — signs showing how loud or soft to play.

Fermata (⌒) — indicates that a note should be held longer than its true value.

Fine — the end.

First time bar (|1.————) — the bars under the bracket are played the 1st time only.

Flat sign (♭) — lowers a note one semitone. Play the next key to the left.

Forte (𝆑) — loud.

Harmonic interval — the interval between two notes sounded together.

Incomplete bar — a bar at the beginning of a piece with fewer counts than shown in the time signatures. The missing counts are found in the last bar.

Interval — the difference in pitch (highness or lowness) between two notes.

Key signature — the number of sharps or flats in any key—written at the beginning of each line.

Legato — smoothly connected. Usually indicated by a slur over or under the notes.

Major scale — a series of 8 notes made of two tetrachords joined by a whole tone.

Melodic interval — the interval between two notes sounded separately.

Mezzo forte (𝆐𝆑) — moderately loud.

Moderato — moderately.

Natural sign (♮) — cancels a sharp or flat.

Octave sign (8va) — when placed OVER notes, means play them one octave higher than written.

Pedal mark (⌐_____⌐) — press the damper pedal, hold it, and release it.

Piano (𝆏) — soft.

Repeat signs — repeat from the beginning.

— repeat the bars between the double bars.

Ritardando (abbreviated ritard. or rit.) — gradually slowing.

Second time bar (|2.————) — the bars under the bracket are played the 2nd time only.

Semitone — the distance from one key to the very next one, with no key between.

Sharp sign (♯) — raises a note one semitone. Play the next key to the right.

Staccato — separated or detached. Usually indicated by a dot over or under the note.

Tempo — rate of speed.

Tetrachord — four notes in alphabetical order, having the pattern of WHOLE TONE, WHOLE TONE, SEMITONE.

Time signatures (𝅘𝅥 2/4, 3/4, 4/4) — numbers found at the beginning of a piece or section of a piece. The top number shows the number of beats in each measure. The bottom number shows the kind of note that gets one beat.

Whole tone — two semitones. The distance between two keys with one key between.

Certificate of Promotion

This is to certify that

_____

has successfully completed Level 1B
of the LESSON BOOK and is hereby promoted
to Level 2 of Alfred's Basic Piano Library.

_____   _____
Date   Teacher